SENIOR HOUSING 101

Your Basic Field Guide
To Understanding Today's
Complex Senior Housing Market

Library of Congress Control Number: 2007905483

ISBN: 978-0-9798497-0-1

Editing by Gabriel D. Gloege
Cover Design and Illustrations by Cantele, Sedivy & Associates Advertising, Inc.
Photograph of Author by Thomas Balsamo

SENIOR HOUSING 101

Your Basic Field Guide
To Understanding Today's
Complex Senior Housing Market

FIRST EDITION

RANDALYNN KAYE, CMP

"Finally somebody has begun to talk honestly about what must change, and what must be left behind, if we are to navigate the living options available in our later years. It is an extraordinary ride. A fact-filled, honest account of dealing with living choices with a born storyteller's gift of observation, experience, and a generous heart. Randalynn Kaye is down to earth and honest and her story entertains while teaching within a compassionate framework. So many people will find this book full of practical advice and will benefit from reading it."

David B. Wolfe, author of *Serving the Ageless Market*, *Ageless Marketing* and co-author of *Firms of Endearment*

"Now there's no need to agonize over the process of finding and choosing the proper housing for elderly loved ones. Randalynn Kaye's years of senior housing experience coupled with her valuable insider 'know-how' will guide you every step of the way. Like a trusted friend leading the way, every detail on the topic of senior housing is covered in this time-saving gem of a book. Be sure to make *Senior Housing 101* your first stop as your travel down the road of senior housing."

Joy Loverde, author of *The Complete Eldercare Planner*
(Random House, 2000)

"*Senior Housing 101* comes at a perfect time when people really need to prepare for their own future since the fastest growing segment of our society is 85 years of age! In order for people to maintain choice in their lives, they must prepare and your book will certainly assist them in this endeavor."

Timothy M. Ruth, J.D.
Vice President, Financial Services Division
Key Financial Group, Inc.

"*Senior Housing 101* is an extraordinary book and valuable tool, written with grace; humor; passion, and always moving. Randalynn Kaye helps the reader clearly see through the maze of senior living options and obstacles. What makes her voice original is how she takes the reader through complex living decisions, making them simple to understand. By combining a talent for seeing and listening with a storytellers gift for clarification, she keeps you interested in the journey and doesn't let go of you until you've said, yes, I see; this is how it is. Here is someone sharing her personal experience and story out of love for the truth and a need to tell it. I highly recommend it!"

Jim Gilmartin
President, Coming of Age, Incorporated

"Seldom does one come across a resource so highly recommendable for both seniors seeking lifestyle and living options, as well as for persons researching possibilities for their aging parents! Comprehensive and compassionate; insightful and wise, Randalynn Kaye's *Field Guide* charts a comforting course through the complex and emotionally charged waters aging adults and adult children navigate when transitioning from one stage of life to the next. Written from the unique perspective and expertise of a senior housing professional as well as loving daughter and daughter-in-law, Kaye's vignettes perceptively illustrate the heart-wrenching and mind-boggling challenges families face. With humor and clarity, she guides the reader through the obstacles and challenges of discernment and decision-making. *Senior Housing 101* serves as a spiritual companion for those seeking to find a haven for restless souls. When the body dwells peacefully, the soul is at rest."

Chaplain Karen Pugliese, M.A., B.C.C.
Chair, Board of Directors, National Association of Catholic Chaplains

"I'm giving this book to colleagues and friends who are constantly being challenged to come up with housing alternatives for older adults. With so many choices finding the right fit can be daunting. In contrast to other senior housing books, *Senior Housing 101* helps move you through the housing options maze in a logical manner. Using her own experience as a springboard, Randalynn Kaye's unique insights make this a rare guidebook that can be read and understood quickly by caregivers."

Lesley Connors, R.N., B.S., M.S., F.C.N.
Director of CNS Home Health & Hospice Parish Nurse Program

"*Senior Housing 101* balances just the right amount of technical information with personal anecdotal stories that make the information come-to-life. As the son of elderly parents (who just this year moved into an independent retirement community), I found this book exceedingly helpful. You make the complexity of the situation much more understandable and subsequently have confidence in making the right decision(s). As a Chaplain and Director of Spiritual Care Resources, I have an affinity for the image of the Good Shepherd. As I read *Senior Housing 101*, I found myself being gently and lovingly shepherded by the words. Not at all a marketing effort to sell a particular product, this book guides the reader on paths that are authentic to the individual. The stated mission is 'empowering individuals with knowledge, insight and resources to successfully navigate lifestyle and aging transitions.' Mission accomplished!"

Chaplain Rod Accardi, D. Min.
Director of Spiritual Care Resources & Volunteer Services
Central DuPage Hospital

"This exceptional publication charts a road map for success in considering alternatives regarding the future housing and healthcare needs as one grows older. It is also a great way for the sons and daughters of aging parents to understand and provide support during the journey. Written with practical ideas, thought provoking insights and shared heartfelt moments, *Senior Housing 101* is all that's needed to successfully transition to the next chapter in one's life."

Joseph L. Benson, CASPF
President, Wyndemere Senior Living Campus

"Even though I'm a practicing health care professional, I was woefully unprepared for the tribulations and turmoil of helping my parent during her time of need. Had I done my homework ahead of time, and had *Senior Housing 101* in hand, the task of finding the right resources for my mom would have been so much easier for both of us. The next time someone tells you 'I'm not ready yet' hand them a copy of *Senior Housing 101!*"

Phyllis Thornton
President, Signum

"*Senior Housing 101* is an excellent primer and workbook to help families navigate the long-term-care continuum."

Daniel G. Parsons, Esq.
Certified Elder Law Attorney

"Certainly this is the kind of material that needs to be out there to address the ever widening demand. I should know. My 80-year-old dad had a heart attack right before Christmas and our family is currently assessing all the options. *Senior Housing 101* could not have come to me at a better time."

Mark Trocchi
Exhibits Manager, Association Book Exhibit

"I've watched from afar my closest friends struggling with the unexpected life-altering events that affected every aspect of their parent's lives as well as their own. Both my husband and I are blessed to have parents who are in their mid 80s and living independently. If this were to change, I was not prepared to deal with all that would be presented. *Senior Housing 101* has helped organize my thoughts and prepare for the unknown in a logical and non-threatening fashion. It is a wonderful resource for adult children with aging parents!"

Kelli Vestal, M.A., C.C.C.
Director of Rehabilitation Services, Central DuPage Hospital

"*Senior Housing 101* is an excellent piece and will be helpful to many."

Rev. Dr. John Rodgers
United Church of Christ

"*Senior Housing 101* is a must read for all caregivers faced with the challenge of helping their aging loved ones navigate their housing and lifestyle options. This book provides clear answers to the many questions and concerns that adult children have when faced with the role reversal of now caring for their parents. Randalynn Kaye, who has extensive experience in the field of senior housing as well as first hand experience assisting her own parents, has taken a complex interpersonal and financial situation and provided important information with sensitivity, wisdom and insight."

Christine Crosby
Editorial Director, GRAND Magazine

"Randalynn Kaye has beautifully blended a primer on the senior living industry with a guide to tour the options and key questions one should address when planning to get the most from life's second half. The material is both comprehensive and easy to understand due to a masterful use of colloquial language bringing reality to the material and making tough topics less threatening. Both the text and the worksheets are an exceptional resource for anyone planning a late-life move to their next home. *Senior Housing 101* also guides the children of aging parents in their role as either caring consultant or concerned caregiver."

G. Richard Ambrosius
Vice President of Communications, Coaching & Culture, Praxeis

"*Senior Housing 101* is very informative and helpful. I am giving this book to our clients as they help their family members with lifestyle transitions. I highly recommend this useful tool to anyone interested in assisting their loved ones!"

Jennifer Prell
President, A Silver Connection, Inc. and Paxem, Inc.

In memory of my father

Kenneth W. Schultz

whose life and death inspired me

Table of Contents

So... What's Your Situation?

You're probably reading this book because you or a loved one is starting to have concerns about living alone. For an elderly individual or a couple, living alone can become difficult, and even dangerous, for any number of reasons:

- Dad shouldn't be mowing the lawn or cleaning the gutters.
- Mom's having trouble going up and down the stairs.
- Driving at night has become dangerous.
- A declining memory is having trouble remembering certain appointments.

Or maybe it's more severe. Perhaps Mom had a fall, or Dad's become ill, and suddenly the tasks and chores of maintaining their current lifestyle have become overwhelming.

Whatever the reason, you sense it's time for a change, but you're not sure what that change should be...or where to begin your research.

That's what this book is for. It lays out the fundamental landscape of senior housing and helps you understand the options whether for yourself or your aging parents or relatives. It will explain the different types of living available, discuss the pros and cons of each, and provide you with a formula to make the important and sometimes difficult decisions that must balance lifestyle, finance, values, health and safety, and more.

In short, after reading this book you will be an educated consumer of the senior housing market. You will know how to…

- Compare housing choices and find the best fit for you or your loved one
- Understand the various financial options and contracts
- Research and ask questions
- Make sense of the terminology used in the senior housing industry
- Evaluate the risk and value factors in making your decision

Knowing these things will allow you to easily separate the wheat from the chaff. And in doing so you'll avoid wasting hours of your precious time, reduce the stress of this emotionally charged life transition, and possibly save hundreds or thousands of dollars in the process.

Here's What You'll Learn

This book has been divided into several sections, each important to becoming a savvy consumer and making the best choices for your particular situation. First we'll identify the main issues and problems that lead to making this type of a life change and give you a brief overview of the options available in today's market.

Next we'll discuss the "facts of life" in today's market so you understand the standard process and paths typically taken through different stages of life and care, as well as some important paradigms and perceptions that influence the research process.

Then we'll introduce the formula for your success. This balances the critical factors that must be considered when researching and deciding what the most appropriate next step is for your situation. And, if used properly, it will shave time and stress off your research process, saving you considerable dollars when you do make a decision.

After that I'll explore each of the primary options for senior housing available in today's ever-changing market. Here we'll evaluate the pros and cons of each option, weigh the cost-to-benefit ratios, discuss the important questions you need to ask, explain the different types of contracts available, and more.

Finally, I'll leave you with plenty of research notes. These are specific exercises, questions, and recommendations—most of which you can do right away—that will jumpstart your research and put you on the road to making the best decision you can for you or your loved ones. And, as a bonus, I've included a glossary and list of additional resources to help expand your search.

But before we get into any of that, you're probably asking yourself, "Who is this person, and why should I listen to her?"

Been There. Done That.

Allow me to properly introduce myself. My name is Randalynn Kaye and I've been in the senior housing industry for nearly 10 years as a sales and marketing professional. In that time I've met and worked with hundreds of adult children and their elderly parents who had decided to leave their home and make a lifestyle change. I've also been on the "consumer side" of the journey, helping manage the relocation to senior housing of my own parents as well as my husband's. It is an emotionally charged transition and helping people through this decision time and process has become something of a passion for me.

For several years now, many of my friends and co-workers have been asking me for advice on issues with their aging parents. "Where do I go?" "I know nothing about this topic." "How do I understand all the options and differences as I look at communities?" "How do I talk to my parents about this?" "What questions do I need to ask?" And for several years I've done what I can to help them.

Over the years I've realized that the average person—whether 70 to 90 years old and looking for themselves, or 30 to 70 years old and looking for their aging parents, grandparents, or loved ones—has no place to go to get a clear, basic understanding of senior housing options. What people need is information that will save them time and energy and help them be more effective with their research.

Taking complex ideas and breaking them down so they can be easily understood is something I've always enjoyed...and the senior housing marketplace can be a complex and confusing place. So that's what I've tried to do with this book. Two quick notes before going forward...

First, I've written this book as though addressing the adult child—most likely the 40 to 60 year old "baby boomer" who is trying to navigate this labyrinth to help their aging parent(s). Regardless of whether you are starting this search for yourself or your parents, the information that follows will be a valuable guide. Use this as a workbook...mark it up, take notes, highlight information, make it yours.

Second, this information focuses primarily on Independent Living, though I do explain the basics of Assisted Living and Skilled Nursing to help jumpstart your research in those areas. If those terms sound foreign to you right now, don't worry...they won't by the time you're half way through this book.

Now, let's get down to business.

When Is It Time For A Change?

This is often a difficult question to answer. Changing the lifestyle your parents have become so familiar with can be daunting, and it's understandable why many people I work with have a hard time identifying that a change is needed. In my experience I have seen three primary reasons people choose to take that next step.

#1 – The Health-Related Wake-Up Call

Sol and Rachel had led a very successful life. He was a retired attorney; they had raised 3 children, downsized from the big family home and now lived in a townhouse. One evening Sol fell down the basement steps. Fortunately he was not seriously injured...but the fall was their health-related wake-up call. "Maybe we shouldn't be trying to manage all these stairs," they said to themselves. The fall told them it was time for a change.

Another couple, Tony and Rose, decided they needed to leave their home when Tony began demonstrating the early stages of memory loss. Rose knew that, as his needs increased, she couldn't handle caring for him and maintaining the house as well.

Several years after losing her husband, Lois had a stroke. She survived and was doing very well, but living alone and not knowing what the future held concerned her. She knew it would be best to think about some different lifestyle options, so she started her research process.

As these examples illustrate, the health-related wake-up call is an event or situation that gets someone's attention. It's a crisis or change that doesn't force a person into assisted living or skilled nursing care, but makes them think about the future. The adult children often see it way before their parents, while older adults will sometimes view the episode as something they just need to "get over"…like a bad cold. Some people will even remain in denial until a more serious crisis occurs.

The most common health-related wake-up calls I see are:

- A fall
- A stroke or TIA (mini-stroke)
- The early diagnosis of memory loss
- Cancer or Parkinson's that is still manageable
- Macular Degeneration or changing eyesight

If your parents experience something like this, it is time for ACTION! Even if your parents are in denial or resisting the idea of making a move, the adult child must know what the options are and start gathering information.

#2 – Difficulty Maintaining Current Home

Cliff and Eunice had been blessed with excellent health. They were traveling extensively, working out and enjoying their grandchildren… generally being active, engaged, and productive well into their later years. Then the roof started to leak, the dryer conked out, the snow removal service didn't show up after a foot of snow came down, their property taxes were climbing…in short, maintaining their well-loved home was becoming a hassle.

This common dilemma sends many people out to start their research. When the challenge of maintaining a home outweighs the pleasure and relaxation you get from living there, it's time to change. Sometimes trying to maintain the home is what leads to the "health-related wake-up call"…Dad falls off the ladder trying to clean the gutters or getting to the attic, Mom falls trying to take out the trash or carry a load of laundry to the basement.

One of the most difficult things to do in an emotionally charged situation is to introduce logic. Sometimes addressing the logic and reality of trying to maintain a home is what will get people off the dime and starting to face the fact that they need to move. Later on I'll give you plenty of tips on how to do this.

#3 – Desire to be Close to Family & Friends

Many people reach a point in life when it becomes more important to be close to their real support system. Fritz and Hilda, my husband's parents, for instance, had been in the same town for well over 50 years. They were familiar with everything and very resistant to a move or any changes. German, stubborn, and survivors of the war, there seemed to be no budging them.

> # Fun Fact:
> For the first time in history, the number of people aged 60 years or over will soon surpass those under 5.

Eventually the house became too much to handle, and after looking at options in the Philadelphia area we had a family pow-wow and laid out the facts. Their only son, my husband, lived in Chicago and he was their primary (and in most cases their only) support system. Even though it meant an uncomfortable change, knowing that he was near to help them if something happened eventually outweighed their fear of change and the upheaval of a move.

Often people will retire to places like Florida, Arizona, or the Carolinas to be near the golf course or the beach where it's warm and sunny. But at some point that all becomes secondary to being close to the ones they love…their sons, daughters, grandchildren and great-grandchildren.

The flip side of the coin is the person who has children spread all over the country and decides to stay put in their familiar geographical surroundings or perhaps a person with no family. If financially viable, positioning themselves in a continuing care retirement community is a good option.

The Top Three Questions Seniors Ask Themselves

As we age, there are three questions that, consciously or not, dance around in the back of our minds.

1. What happens if I get sick?
2. What quality of services do I hope to receive?
3. Do I have enough money to last me the rest of my life?

Doing the homework outlined in this book and starting your research will help you and your loved ones understand the answers to those three questions and ultimately feel more at peace with the decisions you make.

How Will You Decide?

Everyone makes their decisions about senior housing lifestyles differently, and each situation is unique. However, senior housing professionals have come to recognize four main types of consumer.

The Advance Planner: This is the person who starts their research early, taking their time to become an educated consumer and exploring all the options that are available. Usually this type of person is not afraid of the tough questions, willing to discuss end-of-life issues, and engage in deep, meaningful conversations with loved ones. The advanced planner is the one who makes a move before they have to and stays in control of the process.

The Reluctant Consumer: This person is somewhat reluctantly pulled into the research process by their spouse or adult children. They really don't want to have to face the idea of making changes in their lives, but grudgingly participate in the process.

The Wake-Up Call: This is the person who finally concedes to make a move after a near crisis: when the health challenge cannot be denied any longer and a change must happen. If the person is fortunate, they may still be capable of functioning in an independent living community.

The Scrambler: This is the person who suffers a more serious health challenge that necessitates an immediate move. It usually involves family making all the choices because the older adult can no longer handle processing the options or changes. Most times it involves moving directly into assisted living or skilled nursing care.

Unfortunately I sometimes experience seniors that choose to put their head in the sand and play ostrich about their aging process, thinking they are staying in control of their lives, when the reality is just the opposite. Then, when a serious crisis occurs, someone else will have to scramble around and make the decisions for them as to where they will live and who will care for them.

The wonderful thing is we are all "at choice" in life and each person can choose how they want to approach this aspect of their journey. So the question to ask yourself or your loved ones is... How will you decide?

Key Points to Remember...

- Most people make a change for one of three common reasons: they experience a health-related wake-up call; they have difficulty maintaining their current home or they have a desire to be closer to family and friends.

- When contemplating a change, people are usually most concerned with these three questions: What happens if I get sick? What quality of services do I hope to receive? Do I have enough money to last me the rest of my life?

- Senior housing professionals have come to recognize four main types of consumer: The Advance Planners, The Reluctant Consumers, The Wake-Up Call, The Scrambler. Which one will you be?

Concepts First...

Before we explain what options are out there to explore, let's take moment to break down two basic concepts that will make everything easier to understand. All the options we'll discuss will fall into one of two general categories.

Traditional Real Estate which may include:

- Remaining at home
- Down Sizing into an apartment, townhouse, condo, or smaller house
- Moving in with family
- Moving into an Active Adult Community

A Retirement Community which may include:

- A Rental Retirement Community
- A Continuing Care Retirement Community
- A Retirement Community setting with limited services

A majority of Retirement Community settings consist of apartment homes, but may also include single-story townhouses, villas, cottages, and other layouts. Regardless of the type of building, these communities are essentially independent living in a more "user friendly" environment for adults 62 and over.

The floor plans and sizes will vary greatly, ranging from a modest Studio or one-bedroom apartment home to a townhouse or villa floor plan that's well over 2,000+ square feet and may include a basement and attached garage. By design, a Retirement Community will provide more safety, security, socialization, and life enrichment opportunities that are often sought by older adults. Most Retirement Community settings will include some or all of the following services and amenities for residents that can make life easier as a person ages.

- Utilities (often heating, A/C, water, trash removal, etc.) and perhaps cable TV service

- Maintenance of the home (often including the appliances and infrastructure like heating, air-conditioning, and plumbing)

- Maintenance of the grounds (including landscaping and snow removal) and maintenance of all the common areas in the building or on the campus

- Security, emergency alert systems, sometimes a nurse or health center is available during business hours

- Courtesy transportation

- Housekeeping services

- Flexible Dining Options such as one or two meals a day being served in a dining room or various venues to choose from like a Bistro, Café, Buffet, etc.

- Activities and life enrichment programs

- Enhanced Common Areas: This can range from just a few to all the 'bells and whistles'! These enhancements again provide easy and convenient access for residents to enjoy and enrich their living experience at the community and may include: Library, Hair Salon, Convenience Store, Greenhouse, Card and Game Room, Auditorium or Community Room, Private Dining Room, Cocktail Lounge, Theater, Swimming Pool, Spa, Fitness Center, Business Center, Computer Lab, Art Studio, Music Room, Meeting and Class Rooms, Putting Green or Golf Course, Garden Plots, Concierge Services, Chapel or Meditation Room, etc.

As you can see, Retirement Communities these days sound more like a vacation resort than the "old folks home" many people still envision.

Options To Explore and Understand

Once the realization is made that a change of lifestyle is necessary, you need to begin exploring the options. And what are those options? While the senior housing market is vast and ever-changing, below is a brief summary of the most common options to explore, each one will be discussed in detail later on.

Make no changes, stay in home: This is a viable option and needs to be carefully evaluated. Some people will put a qualifier on the decision, e.g. until I need assisted living, until I can't drive, until my spouse dies. Even if your parents decide this option is best, they should re-evaluate it periodically as changes occur in life to be sure it is still the best and safest option.

Downsize to smaller home: Another option to explore may be to simply unload the larger home and downsize to a smaller home, apartment, condominium, or townhouse. You need to consider how old your parents are and how many times do they want move.

Move in with family: I'll mention this when I'm presenting to a large audience and it always draws laughter and moans… usually in equal proportion. Though most people in this day and age would prefer not to do this, it is an option that many families embrace. It may need to be seriously considered for financial reasons. Others accept this as part of their cultural or family traditions.

Move to an Active Adult Community: Active Adult Communities for ages 55+ are popping up all over the country. As the first wave of baby-boomers turn 60, they hope to capture this massive wave of aging America. An Active Adult Community will be the same as traditional real estate, but with access to senior-oriented activities and without teenagers or toddlers living next door.

Move to a Retirement Community: The differences in retirement communities will be around how they are paid for and what, if any, future long-term care services may be included. The setting will be designed with the aging process in mind—grab rails in the tub/shower areas, no stairs, wider doorways for walkers, wheelchairs, or scooters, etc. The community may include apartment homes, townhouses with all living and laundry on one floor, or variations of the lifestyle called villas, cottage homes, duplexes, or the like. The verbiage may change but the concept remains the same. The most common types of Retirement Communities are:

- The Rental Retirement Community: The resident pays for the cost of living in the community on a month-to-month rental basis. The community may have just independent living or it may also have assisted living and/or long-term care. The defining factor here is that the resident pays rent.

- The Continuing Care Retirement Community (CCRC): "Continuing Care" means there is Independent Living, Assisted Living, and Skilled Nursing care all on the same campus or in the same building (we'll talk about each of those in just a minute). Most frequently the consumer will find the CCRC requires an up-front investment, often referred to as an Entrance Fee, and a recurring Monthly Fee that includes services and amenities. This option involves various types of contracts referred to as "Residency Agreements" and is usually the most complex for the consumer to grasp.

- The Retirement Community with limited services: There continue to be many new versions of the retirement community lifestyle springing up in the market with variations on the how the resident pays and what they get for what they pay. Many times they will look and feel similar to the models mentioned above, but simply have fewer services. This may include some enhanced common areas but perhaps no 24-hour security, no staff or transportation on weekends, no healthcare components, etc.

Invest in Long Term Care Insurance...
A consideration for any of the above options

Regardless of what housing option is the best fit, you may want to consider Long Term Care Insurance in the research. Long Term Care Insurance is a very hot topic in the market place right now, mostly targeting the 78 million baby-boomers. I'll address some basic information about this topic later on, but first let me make clear that I am not a long term care insurance expert. I have helped many people figure it into their risk and value equation and understand how to compare costs and benefits to some of the Retirement Community options. The bottom line on long term care insurance is the younger and healthier you are when you invest in it, the more reasonable the cost. Also understanding what you get for what you invest and how it fits in to other options needs to be evaluated as part of the research process.

The Facts of Life...Today

In starting your research you need to establish a baseline of information about how our society works regarding care for the elderly. So let's talk for a moment about one of my favorite people... Ethel Mertz. (If you don't know who Ethel is, ask your parents or grandparents!)

Let's say that Ethel lives independently in her house and has for many years. If she wanted to, Ethel could move to an Independent Living retirement community and continue enjoying her independent lifestyle in a more senior-oriented environment. Her path would look like this:

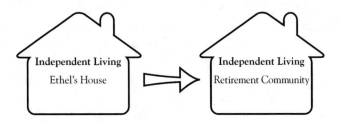

But Ethel has no intention of ever moving. She is fond of saying, "If I leave this house, it'll be feet first!" So she stays in her home until a major health crisis occurs. Once this happens, the family and doctor say, "Ethel, you can't live in your house any longer… you simply must move directly to a higher level of care."

At this point Ethel will bypass any independent living retirement community option and, in most cases, move directly to Assisted Living. Her path will look like this:

Assisted Living is designed for the person who is not able to live independently, but does not need 24-hour nursing care; it is independent living with assistive services as necessary. Such services will include three meals a day, assistance with bathing and dressing, medication reminders, and more. These are referred to as ADLs, or Activities of Daily Living. The number of ADLs a person needs assistance with will determine the costs and level of service.

For right now I'm not going into greater detail about Assisted Living, but you should know one thing… Medicare does NOT pay for the cost of Assisted Living. Depending on what part of the country Ethel lives in and the level of service needed, she will pay approximately $4,000 to $6,000 per month for Assisted Living.

If Ethel's health declines, she will eventually need Skilled Nursing Care. For this she will move to what used to be called a nursing home, though the politically correct term now is a Skilled Nursing Facility. Sometimes referred to as a SNF ("sniff"), this is more of a medical environment. Her path now looks like this:

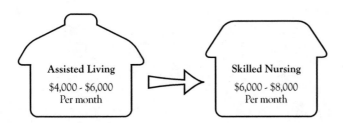

If Ethel meets the Medicare criteria, a combination of her Medicare insurance and her supplemental health insurance will usually pay for the first 100 days for her care. After the 100 days has expired, Ethel will then have to pay $6,000 to $8,000 per month for Skilled Nursing Care. When she has spent down most of her assets, Ethel then applies for Medicaid, which is the state-operated welfare system.

If the health crisis was serious enough to require Ethel to have 24-hour nursing care, she would bypass independent living in a retirement community setting, bypass assisted living, and go directly into a skilled nursing facility.

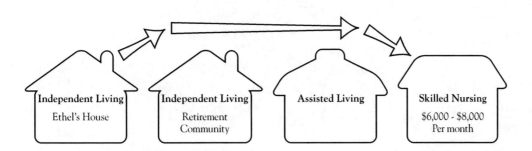

So there you have it. Independent Living, Assisted Living, and Skilled Nursing Care are the three major components of elder care that shape today's senior housing market. There are finer details, of course, and missing pieces of the picture for everyone, but keep in mind there are no right or wrong answers about the next step in one's journey through life… after all, no one has a crystal ball!

Some people are fine staying in their home and peacefully complete their journey on this earth with few or no complications. Others may require years of assisted living or skilled nursing care. It all boils down to a decision about Risks and Values, which will come to light, as you continue your research. We'll discuss these risks and values later, but first I want to talk about the mental side of starting your research.

Paradigms and Perceptions

One of the most challenging aspects of the research and decision making process is often the mindset of the older adult. I've seen adult children beside themselves with frustration because mom or dad refuses to even discuss making a change. When I present to a large group, I know there are at least a handful of people in the audience that have been reluctantly dragged to the "Lunch and Learn" by their spouse or family member.

Take a look at the picture below.

Do you see an old man with long hair and a grizzly beard, or two young lovers kissing under an arbor? Whichever you see depends on your perspective.

It is the same when a person approaches this research. Some individuals will be close-minded, negative, and reluctant at best. Others will be more open and enjoy the learning and exploration process.

Mr. Valle was an engineer who was educated in the United States, spent most of his life building hydroelectric dams in his native Bolivia, and returned to America for retirement. He had a very large family, and when it was time for him to make a change, his daughter, Maria, lead the research and organized a family visit to my community.

When all 10 of them showed up, one of Mr. Valle's sons walked right up to me and defiantly exclaimed, "My father isn't going to live in some old folks home!" I assured him I didn't want that for his father either, and encouraged him to temporarily suspend his assumptions until he'd finished the tour. Forty-five minutes later the whole family—including the fiery son—was buzzing about which apartment he should have, how to arrange the furniture, and how much he was going to enjoy all the activities. Talk about a 180!

The point of this story is that senior housing as a whole has shifted considerably more toward the hospitality industry and away from the old "medical models" many people still picture in their minds. And this trend will only continue. However, some older adults (and even their children) are stuck in the old paradigm of the "old folks home"…usually a lonely, dreary 1950s version of a nursing home that no one would want to live in!

To get someone out of this old paradigm they need to see, feel, touch and experience the options available to them. If you're dealing with someone who needs a paradigm shift, start with the least threatening step. Go out and gather some collateral materials, look at websites, ask some non-threatening open-ended questions to begin a dialog. I'll give you plenty of tips later on. But for now just remember, approaching the research process with an open mind will have a major impact on your ultimate success.

Notes:

Key Points to Remember…

- Senior living options fall into essentially two categories: Traditional Real Estate or a Retirement Community.

- With traditional real estate you could choose to stay in your own home, downsize to a smaller home, move in with family, or move to an active adult community.

- Retirement Community options include Rental Retirement Communities, Continuing Care Retirement Communities, or Retirement Communities with limited services.

- Today's senior living marketplace offers three distinct levels of care that are accepted and understood throughout the industry: Independent Living, Assisted Living, and Skilled Nursing Care.

- Our paradigms and perceptions can affect our outlook dramatically. Be sure to keep yours open and focused on the learning process and you may just find a diamond that you previously thought was a lump of coal.

Your Formula for Success

It's important to understand that making a lifestyle change is an investment, both financially and emotionally. As with any investment, you want to do your due diligence. Many other fields of investment use formulas to help guide this research. A real estate investor looks at things like rental income, location, and down payment. A new car buyer has to consider gas mileage, financing terms, warranties, and so on.

And so it is when looking at senior housing options. The tested and proven formula I'm about to provide will help you quickly sort out the options and focus on the issues YOU need to consider when making a decision. Follow the steps below, do the homework before you start looking, and you'll avoid wasting time and energy or feeling confused and frustrated.

> **Fun Fact:** An average American will spend about 6 months of their life waiting at stop lights.

The formula to follow is this:

Risks and Values + Health + Finances = Your Best Option

Let's look at each one individually and see how it all fits together.

Risks and Values: What are you comfortable with?

This is what I call the "internal research"…the soul searching, if you will. Though it may be tricky to get started, this can lead to wonderfully rich conversations that are a gift to the entire family.

Some families naturally engage in this type of dialog. But without prompting, most do not. Many adult children assume they know how their parents feel about some of these questions, when in reality, after deeper discussions, they find it's quite the opposite.

The Risks and Values questions can also be great conversation starters with aging parents who resist even talking about making a move, let alone where, when, and how. If you find yourself in this situation, the following story may be of benefit.

Early one Saturday morning, many years ago, my husband and I were lying in bed when our then 3-year-old son wandered in and asked, in complete earnest, "Dad, am I old enough to screw?"

My husband and I stared at each other for a moment as he cleared his throat and quickly tried to think of how best to explain the birds and the bees to someone so young. "My word!" I thought, "I know they're growing up fast these days...but 3 years old!?!"

I decided to probe a bit first. "Now, honey, what exactly do you mean?"

"Well," he explained, "I know I'm old enough to hammer. But am I old enough to screw?" He was simply asking if he could use Dad's screwdriver!

The point here is this: Seek first to understand, and then be understood. Until Mom and Dad are enthusiastic and excited about exploring a lifestyle change (or at least be agreeable to it) you're going to have your work cut out for you. If you're dealing with difficult loved ones, start by trying to understand the deeper thoughts and feelings of the person who needs to make a change. Even if they disagree with you at first, they will probably be more willing to listen to your suggestions if they feel they've had a chance to be heard first. Try asking your parents some of the following questions to help get the dialog started.

How many times do you want to move? Moving at any age is extremely stressful... physically, mentally and emotionally. That stress may include excitement, joy, relief, anticipation, and more. But the older we are, the more challenging the process will be and the more responsibility will fall on family members to handle the physical aspects of the move. So they should ask themselves, "How many more time do I want to do this?" "Am I better off positioning myself for whatever the future holds?" I encourage families to look at the age and health factors when contemplating this question.

How much space do you actually need? My husband and I downsized from a large home much earlier than most baby-boomers and went into a lovely townhouse. As our nest emptied we began to realize that even though we have eight different rooms plus a basement, we really only live in four of them on a daily basis—the kitchen, great room, master bedroom and office. Take a serious look at how much space your parents really use. Then ask what happens to the rest of the space. Usually it's a collection place for "stuff"!

Making a lifestyle change will usually be a downsizing process. One of the most common issues I hear people wrestle with is having a guest room. So I ask how often they have out of town guests. Usually the response is "not very often". Space is also a very personal consideration. I've had couples come from a modest size home and be very content with a small one-bedroom apartment, and I've had a single person come from a 6,000 square foot home and downsize to a 2,000 square foot townhouse and feel squeezed for space.

So have them reflect on how much space they really need, and what is most important for them to do with that space. If they are considering a move to an independent living retirement community, find out what common spaces are available that function as an extension of the home, such as a guest suite, a private dining room, a grand piano, a business center, a library. They may not need to recreate all these spaces if they exist for use in the community.

Is home maintenance causing worry or stress? Have them think back over the last several years at the time, energy, and money they've spent trying to maintain their home. Is it becoming more bothersome, a point of stress, eating up valuable time and energy in their life? Also look at what will have to be maintained or improved within the next five years… new roof, painting, heating and air conditioning, gutters, windows. At what point is it no longer worth trying to keep it up? When is it time to simplify or unload what has become a burden?

Do you have safety concerns? Take a close look at your parents' home environment. Though they may have lived there many years and are familiar with the environment, little things have a way of creeping in over time. Do they have to climb stairs to get to the bedrooms or a bathroom? Is the driveway on a slope that may be dangerous to navigate in winter weather? Are they carrying laundry baskets up and down the basement stairs? Do they still climb a ladder to store things in the attic?

Roy and Edith lived on a beautiful acreage where they had gardened for years, raised their family, and put a lot of creativity into their lovely home. Though close to 80 years old and slowing down, they still felt they could manage just fine. One afternoon Roy was storing things in the attic space above their garage and fell straight backwards off the ladder. It took an entire year to recuperate from that fall. Only then did they both have the strength and mental energy to process making a move into a retirement community setting.

The goal is to make a change before the accident happens, so carefully reflect on safety concerns that you and your parents currently have or may become greater concerns in the future.

Are you still comfortable with your neighborhood? In 1959, when my husband was a child, his parents moved into a charming little three-bedroom home on a two-lane road, near forest preserves and apple orchards in a suburb of Philadelphia. As the years passed, the two-lane road became a four-lane highway, and the demographics began to change along with the condition of the homes and shopping along their road. His parents lived through all these slow changes and thought nothing of it. They were in a familiar surrounding. They were in their comfort zone. When my husband and I would visit we'd realize how much the area was changing and we encouraged them to think about moving.

Do you expect to live with your children? In today's fast-paced, mobile society where often both spouses work full time and keep hectic family schedules, it's much less common to see aging parents moving in with their children. Each family may view this option differently. For some it is impossible, for others it may be a financial necessity, and for others it may be a family tradition. Regardless of where you're coming from, it is another option. Be sure you know how both you and your parents feel about the idea and whether to explore it in more detail as part of your research.

Are you concerned about being a burden to your children, family, or friends? A majority of older adults will tell me they absolutely do NOT want to be a burden to anyone. This again is one of those delicate areas where timing is key. Some are advance planners and position themselves before serious issues start to occur; others wait until there has been an episode or two, then begin to get the picture.

When my father-in-law had open heart surgery, my husband had to take vacation time, fly out to Pennsylvania and oversee the care, transition home and be sure they could handle the follow-up rehab and doctor visits before returning. This happened several times with various emergencies... yet they remained obstinate and determined to stay in their home where there was no local family support to respond to these emergencies. It was a burden. And while we tried to present our concerns diplomatically and still honor their wishes and independence, it made both my husband and me angry that they didn't "get it".

This is not an uncommon situation for many adult children, and it can be a challenging discussion for some families to have. It is best when everyone concerned—parents, children, relatives that may have to oversee care—are all participating so all perspectives and feelings are put on the table and heard. Like other risk/value factors, there usually comes a point that a person feels strong enough about NOT being a burden, that they are willing to make a change.

Who is your support system? If there was a major crisis in your parent's life, if the bottom fell out and they couldn't handle the situation, if they were seriously ill or going to die... who is their support system? Who would they call? Who would be there to support them, care for them, be an advocate for them or handle their affairs? Some people don't even want to think about this question. They prefer to deny that anything that serious will ever happen to them. It may happen to others, but certainly it won't happen to them! Well, like the ad on TV says... life comes at you fast! It is seldom what you plan for, rarely what you expect, and sometimes beyond what you ever dreamed might happen.

When my father had a serious stroke, my mother kept saying, "It just happened so fast. I can't believe it!" Actually, my father's health had been failing for years. He smoked nearly his entire life; he had been falling and having circulation problems. Even though my brothers and I were not surprised to hear of the stroke, it certainly wasn't what my parents expected or planned for. Overnight the support system and family dynamics took a 180-degree shift! Suddenly I was the one who was helping them navigate the health care system, plan the relocation, find a new doctor, and so on.

Making these changes in the midst of a crisis is difficult at best, so look carefully at this question. Being geographically close to that support system will have more value and priority in your parent's life with each passing year. Make sure they know who their support system is and trust it will be there for them no matter what, willing and able to take on the challenges that may be part of their journey.

What if you could no longer drive? For some older adults, no longer being able to drive is a defining moment and prompts a change in lifestyle. If someone lives in an urban setting and has always used public transportation, this is probably not an issue. But for a person in a rural or suburban setting where transportation is required just to cope with the basics of life, it has a significant impact. If your parents could no longer drive, would they (or you!) need to move? Could they rely on family and friends for transportation? How would this impact their social or recreational life?

If something happened to you, what about your spouse? Some couples prefer to wait until something happens to one of them before a change is made. Despite our efforts, my own in-laws refused to leave their house and move geographically closer to us. When we discussed this question, the answer was always that if one of them dies the other would come to live close to us. After four years of diplomatic and not-so-diplomatic discussion, my father-in-law finally admitted the house was too much for them to care for and agreed to move. We were delighted to finally have the opportunity to share our lives with them and be a family, enjoying Sunday dinners and holidays together, getting to really know each other at this time in our lives.

But it was too little too late. That winter my father-in-law caught pneumonia and died a week before the moving van was scheduled to pull up to their door. It was a sad and difficult time for us and might have been prevented had they moved closer to their support system sooner. But we got through it and my mother-in-law moved out near us soon afterward. Since then she's realized how much they missed by not moving when they first had the chance.

In some situations the surviving spouse is perfectly capable and comfortable managing the home alone. Nonetheless, it's wise to get everyone's perspective on this question as well…husbands, wives, and children may all have a different view of the situation.

How important is it to make your own choices? It's human nature to want to feel in control of our lives. Keep in mind however, there are many different ways of maintaining control and different tools to use. My father-in-law chose not to give anyone power of attorney because he was convinced that he would then lose control of his financial affairs. As it turned out, the reality was nearly the opposite. His pneumonia left him in the ICU on a respirator and unconscious without control of anything whatsoever!

So again…life can come at you fast. If it is important for your parents to make their own choices and have a sense of staying in control of their life, then advance planning is mandatory. The person who chooses to put their head in the sand, take no action, refuse to discuss the reality of their aging. and THINKS they are staying in control will likely wake up one day all alone, in a strange place, unable to care for themselves or have a say in where they are living. But the advance planner who understands their options and positions themselves prior to a crisis will have the most control and opportunity to make their own choices.

How attached are you to your "stuff"? A person's "stuff" can paralyze them as they begin to contemplate a life transition. The longer your parents have been in their home, the older they are, the more stressful the very idea of cleaning up, throwing out, down-sizing, reorganizing, and moving can be. I've worked with people so unattached to their stuff they make a lifestyle change by getting all new furniture. I've also worked with people so convinced they have to hang on to their stuff that they refuse to take action…even when evidence that a change is necessary is staring them in the face.

Fear of change is a powerful force, and telling someone to start weeding things out sooner rather than later is like preaching to an overweight person the virtues of a healthy diet and exercise. For some people, bringing in a professional organizer or someone that is unemotionally attached to the "stuff" can make it easier. As part of your research, you must help your parents come to grips with how much power their "stuff" has over them and how they plan to deal with it.

How important is it to be located near children or family? For some families, this is a non-issue. Others struggle with multiple children spread around the country, climate, grandchildren, cost of living, likelihood of the children being transferred or moving with their careers, and so on. Make sure you understand the family dynamics involved, both geographically and emotionally.

Some families will research several geographical locations at one time in an effort to get to the right answer. Many times it boils down to which adult child is best equipped (mentally, emotionally, and physically) to be the primary person to oversee the aging process. If there are no children or family members that can or want to take on this role, that may have a significant impact on the direction of your research.

If left alone, can you maintain your current lifestyle? For married couples, these are often deep and meaningful conversations. Whenever a woman calls my office and tells me her husband refuses to discuss making a move and that she's worried, I always encourage her to be proactive on her own. The first step is to empower herself with knowledge and understanding. And this goes for husbands too.

Encourage your parents to just learn about their options and give some thought to the "what ifs" that life may present. Are they physically and financially able to maintain their current lifestyle? Would they even want to? Their answers may change over time, but they should start where they are now and explore their thoughts and feelings.

Would you prefer to make a lifestyle transition by yourself or do it as a couple while you are able? Many couples will discuss the likelihood that something will happen to one of them before the other. Do they want to make a move together? That way if something happens to one of them, the other isn't left with the house and the "stuff", trying to manage the transition alone. Or do they prefer to stay where they are and simply cross that bridge when/if they come to it?

It is best when the couple and the rest of the family can agree on a course of action. Sometimes one is reluctant and others gently pull them along in the process. The life-long patterns of the marriage and communication will play a significant part when grappling with this question.

Is it increasingly difficult to get out and socialize or drive at night?
Choosing to no longer drive at night (or losing the ability to do so) will often mark the beginning of changes. If your parents are still in their home and do not drive at night, take a close look at how life has changed for them over the past 3 to 5 years. Like many things in life, the changes creep in so slowly they are hardly noticeable. Yet in reflection you may see some changes:

- Have they stopped some of their favorite activities?

- Do they have fewer social contacts?

- Do they sometimes feel stuck and housebound?

- Are they spending more and more time sitting in front of the television set?

- Do they have less and less to talk about with others?

- Have they become depressed?

Helping your parents gently gain awareness of these possibilities or feelings will feed into their value of a different lifestyle

Health: What level of care is needed?

The state of your parents' health will initially set the direction for your research. Are they capable of living in an independent setting? Do they already require assisted or skilled care? Their health will also play a part in the Risk and Values discussions. So the first thing to do is take a realistic look at your parents' health.

You need to know if they have any health challenges or concerns. You should not only be familiar with their current state of health, but also be projecting 3 to 5 years down the line. It may even be time to go to the doctor with Mom or Dad and get an updated professional assessment to help with planning for the future.

All this will help you to determine what level of care they will require—now and in the near future—and will in most cases immediately focus your research. It will also allow for more meaningful and productive discussions with professionals when you are visiting locations.

Here are a few of the most common health issues for older adults that need to be considered:

- Signs of early memory loss
- Declining vision
- Osteoporosis or spinal stenosis
- Cancer

- Difficulty walking
- Parkinson's Disease
- Cardiac problems
- Pulmonary problems

All of these may seem to be minor issues right now or under control with medication. But in time they will likely change or decline, presenting greater challenges. It is best to understand and prepare for those possibilities. If your parents are blessed with good health, they may have more options than if significant health issues are already present. This is why the earlier they begin looking, the better off they will be.

Money: What do you have to work with?

Now it's time to get a handle on the finances. I have a golden rule with this: "Know Before You Go." What I mean is that you absolutely must know how much money your parents have to work with BEFORE you start looking at specific options. If you go shopping for a car, you need to know if you can shop at the Ford dealership, the Cadillac dealership, or look for a good deal on a second hand vehicle.

What you want to avoid is showing your parents options they fall in love with, only to find out afterwards that they are not financially viable. The numbers I'm going to tell you about are also critical points for the marketing professionals you'll be speaking with, so having them handy will speed up the process and allow you to get more specific information from them.

The information you'll need will fall into two categories: Assets and Income. With Assets, the number you're looking for is your parents' total Net Worth, which is Total Combined Capital Assets less Liabilities. This is the total combined value of all the assets they own, such as:

- Cash
- Savings Accounts
- Checking Accounts
- Money Market Accounts
- Certificates of Deposit
- Stocks and Bonds
- IRAs
- Annuities
- Real Estate
- Cash value of insurance policies

What you should NOT include are things like the car, china and crystal, furniture, etc. These are considered commodities and don't factor into the official financial picture. A good rule of thumb is to not include anything they use for daily living, the primary exception being their current home.

Also, it's not important that each of these areas is specifically broken out. The people you will be dealing with are looking for one bottom-line number. If a portfolio already exists simply get the value of the portfolio. You simply need to know the total asset base you have to work with.

When calculating Income it is important to focus on AVAILABLE income. The actual term used by senior housing professionals is "Total Available Monthly Income." So when doing your calculations, count ALL income, regardless of whether the person is using it now or letting interest and dividends roll into the principal.

The most common sources of income are Social Security and Pensions. Often older adults will live very comfortably on their pension and social security and consider that to be their ONLY income. But to be accurate in your research process, you have to dig deeper and look at the entire picture, adding ALL income into one pot.

Other sources may include:

- Interest and Dividends earned from assets
- IRA Income
- Rental Income

When you have tallied all of the annual income from these sources, add it all up and divide by 12. This number is the Total Available Monthly Income. It doesn't mean they have to spend it or take the payout on it. It just has to exist. What you want to know is how much money is available each month without starting to spend down the asset base.

> For many families, money is a delicate topic. Some families communicate openly about money and finances while others feel it's proper to keep this information private... in some instances not even sharing it with their son or daughter who may have power of attorney. Though it may be an uncomfortable challenge to start these conversations, you have to get to the financial bottom line so you have the facts before you start looking at senior housing.

In the back of this book I have included some quick and simple worksheets to get you started gathering the necessary and valuable financial information. After completing the financial homework you'll have a clear picture on paper to help guide the rest of your research process.

The following financial formula is frequently used by CCRCs across the country as a quick and easy way to determine if a community is a financial fit. Rental Retirement Communities and Retirement Communities with limited services may have different or more liberal financial formulas. I recommend you use it ONLY as a reference point and always consult any community of interest to confirm their method, system, or formula.

$$Assets = Entrance\ Fee\ x\ 2$$

$$Income = Monthly\ Fee\ x\ 1.5$$

So if the Entrance Fee is $100,000, your parents will need at least $200,000 in assets to qualify. Some communities only look for 1.5 times the assets. And if the Monthly Service Fee is $2,000, a person will need to have at least $3,000 a month in Available Monthly Income.

Most independent living retirement communities will require a financial disclosure and approval process. Retirement communities want to be sure a person will be financially comfortable both now and in the future. This means they look for the ability to pay the current monthly service fees plus the fees in the future, knowing they will increase a little each year. A common practice in all Retirement Communities is the option for the adult child or a family member to sign a Guarantor Form in the event the older adult does not have sufficient assets and/or income to meet the community's financial criteria.

Key Points to Remember...

- Your formula for success consists of Risks and Values + Health + Finances

- To get people thinking about their own risks and values, ask how they feel about things like: moving, maintaining their home, safety concerns, being near family and children, driving the car, their "stuff", social contact

- Make an assessment of current health conditions, and then project those 3 to 5 years out. How will they progress or decline?

- When figuring out the financial part of the equation calculate both assets and income, and be sure to do this before you start making visits.

So What Are My Choices?

As we've discussed so far, there are a number of different lifestyle options depending on your parents' state of health and finance. These are the most common options:

- Staying at home
- Downsizing with traditional real estate
- Moving in with family
- Active Adult Community
- Rental Retirement Community
- Continuing Care Retirement Community (CCRC)
- Retirement Community with limited services
- The consideration of Long Term Care Insurance with any of the above choices

Now we're going to cover each of these options in detail.

Staying at home

Sometimes older adults fear a change of lifestyle, and often the thought of having to deal with all the "stuff" they've accumulated over the years is simply overwhelming. For these and other reasons, many older adults simply prefer to stay in their home. It's an attractive choice because it seems to be the path of least resistance. If this is what you are hearing from your parents, then you must look closely at how the following factors may impact this choice either now or at some point in the future.

Aging real estate costs money. This has a way of creeping up on people, so it is important to project the costs to maintain the home, especially if they've been living in it for the last 30 to 50 years. Will they need to replace the roof, the HVAC, water heater, windows, or siding? Will they have to update the kitchen, bathroom, or install ramps as their physical abilities diminish? Home ownership can be expensive! If your parents' plan is to never leave their home, their overall "value" decision needs to consider the possible costs and effort necessary to maintain the property. The key question is this—does their attachment and desire to remain in the home outweigh the effort and cost of maintaining it?

Securing reliable services. If your parents can't maintain the house and property by themselves, what will it cost to bring in the services needed... yard and landscape maintenance, snow removal in the winter, housekeeping, window washing, handyman repairs, cleaning the gutters, a fresh coat of paint, and so on? While these activities are usually a source of fulfillment for a younger home owner, they can turn into an energy draining burden for someone in their 60s and 70s, and downright dangerous for an 80+ individual. Many of my clients share their tales of woe and frustration about waiting for the repairman to show up, or the challenge of finding reliable help, or feeling uncomfortable being alone when strangers come into their home.

On the other hand, when people are still able to do these tasks and chores, it gives them a sense of purpose... they still love gardening, mowing the grass, scrubbing the floors, puttering around the basement or garage. The fine balance comes in understanding when climbing ladders, clipping hedges or painting walls is just not as safe and easy as it used to be. Again, the key is to assess this "value" before the work creates a health challenge!

Driving at night or not driving at all. If your parents could no longer drive, is staying in their home a good option? Consider how they would get to the grocery store, the doctor, the hairdresser, and all the other errands we so easily take for granted when we can hop in the car and go. Who will take them? Who will they need to rely on? Are these services within walking distance or easily accessible with public transportation? Even limiting driving during daylight can impact the lives of your parents. Have they had to cut back on attending concerts, bridge groups, dinner out, or other social and cultural activities?

Low social contact. Fritz and Hilda were a prime example of this. As they curtailed their driving at night, as more of their energy was needed to maintain the home, as their friends began to move out of town or pass away, their social contact started to shrink...and so did they! I began hearing them complain more and more out of boredom, they repeated the same stories, watched more soap operas, and became more sedentary. Research has proven that social contact is as important as exercise in extending the longevity of older adults. Low social contact and isolation is also a common cause for geriatric depression often seen in older adults. So carefully evaluate the reality of how isolated your parent(s) are as they age and factor this into your "value" assessment.

> When my father-in-law died suddenly of pneumonia, we moved my mother-in-law close to us in the suburbs of Chicago and into a retirement community...something we had been planning for the both of them, but too little too late. In her new environment she had to walk down the hall every day, a form of built-in exercise the doctor had tried for years to get her to do! She met new people and had opportunities to take advantage of concerts, lectures, and outings. Though she grieved the loss of her husband of nearly 60 years, she was transformed into a new woman simply due to the change of lifestyle.

The cost of in-home care. There are a host of programs and community based senior services that can help staying in the home more affordable and convenient...Meals-on-Wheels, senior ride services, etc. I could expand on the plethora of avenues to explore, but that would be an entire book of its own! I will suggest that you and your family look closely at home care costs...everything from 24-hour nursing care, full time live-in caregivers, companion services and so on. It is often more costly than you think. Some people say they will stay in their homes and have someone come in to provide services simply because they are too stubborn or afraid to look at other options. Other people must find a way to stay in their home as long as possible for financial reasons.

As part of your research, call around your area and find out what it will cost for care-giving or nursing services. There is no right or wrong answer to any of these choices. Primarily for financial reasons, Mary and Ken, my own parents, stayed in their condo until my father's stroke necessitated a change in the midst of a crisis. There were limited assets to work with and we knew that if his condition continued to decline it might necessitate a Medicaid bed in a skilled nursing facility. Dad was in and out of the hospital, going through rehab, and having home health nursing services (most of which was paid for by Medicare and insurance) before finally dying peacefully at home. After a week of hospice services we were $1,700 out of pocket for a 24/7 caregiver to physically help my family through the ordeal. The missing part of the puzzle for everyone is this: No one has a crystal ball! We can only guess at how the journey will play out and make the best decisions we can with what we know, how we feel, and what we have to work with along the way.

Downsize within traditional Real Estate

Another option to consider is simply downsizing from a larger home to a smaller home. This could be a townhouse, condo, apartment, or ranch style home, all of which I refer to as "traditional real estate".

During the 1980s and 1990s my husband and I played what I fondly call "corporate gypsy"... moving every 2 years while climbing the proverbial corporate ladder. It doesn't matter how old or young you are, it's an exhausting process that only gets more stressful as you age. Once into his or her 70s, a person has to ask themselves how many more times they really want to move.

Fun Fact: Americans move, on average, 12 times during their lifetimes.

Depending on your parents' health and finances, downsizing within traditional real estate may be a good choice. I encourage people to look carefully at this option, especially if there is a strong possibility that in less than 5 years another move may be necessary. Downsizing into traditional real estate will still leave them with the same considerations to evaluate as staying in their home.

Move in with family

Moving in with family may have some real advantages if it can work for your family situation. Financially it is certainly the most conservative option. As with generations throughout history, older adults may participate in the day-to-day activities of family life. They may join in with meal preparation, housekeeping, child-care, homework, and emotional support, often adding the richness of wisdom along the way. Family dynamics are a key factor here. It can be a time of healing, re-connecting, and resolution as it was for my father and I. I've also experienced families that would never consider the option no matter what the circumstances. The Risk and Value discussions mentioned earlier will help everyone shine light on this option.

Move to an Active Adult Community

Active Adult Communities are growing like mushrooms around the country with hopes of cashing in on the aging of the baby-boomers. These are communities for people age 55 and older and similar to traditional real estate but without toddlers or teenagers living next door. Active Adult Communities typically have common areas, activities and social opportunities connected with the community that you won't find in a traditional real estate setting.

Many developers are jumping on this bandwagon. While they hope to attract the person 55 to 60 years old, the reality is that many people wait until much later to look at this option. I've often met with families that just moved mom or dad into an Active Adult Community and a few years later need to move them to a Retirement Community setting with more services and amenities. Like traditional real estate, the health and financial equation will play a major part in determining if an Active Adult Community is a good option.

Move to a Rental Retirement Community

A Rental Retirement Community will offer various pros and cons based on the health, financial and risk/value factors you've established. Here are some of them to include as you process this option:

No up-front investment: The main difference between the Continuing Care Retirement Community and a Rental Retirement Community is that there's no up-front investment or Entrance Fee. If a person is working with more limited assets, a simple month-to-month rental may be a better financial option.

No equity return: Because there is no up-front investment there is no equity returned on the investment of paying monthly rent. Some people look at this the same as renting an apartment versus buying a house.

No financial benefits for future health care costs: While most rental communities are independent living, many will also have some assisted living services, and a few include all the levels of care. A person will simply pay rent each month for the level of services they are receiving. Essentially residents pay only for what they need at the time.

Possible move if higher levels of care are needed: If the independent living rental community does not have Assisted Living and Skilled Nursing Care available, a person must move to yet another facility should they require higher levels of care, most commonly when skilled nursing or memory loss care is needed. This means the adult children are usually in for another search and move experience. If the rental option is the best way for your family to go, I encourage you to plan for such a move in advance.

Lease agreement = easy in and out: Sometimes I'll meet a person who tells me they need to move from their home now, but they plan to relocate again in a year or so when their son retires. I encourage people in this type of situation to look at the Rental Retirement Community option. What I want them to avoid is investing in an Entrance Fee at a CCRC only to have to walk away from a portion of that investment a short time later. Many rental communities will require a one year lease with a "no penalty out" for serious illness or death, making it easy to enter into a rental agreement and get out of it quickly.

Move to a Continuing Care Retirement Community (CCRC)

A Continuing Care Retirement Community refers to a community that has Independent Living, Assisted Living, and Skilled Nursing Care all available on the same campus or, in the case of an urban high-rise setting, in one building. It is designed so the resident moves into the community while still functioning on an independent level, and within this very "user friendly" environment they are now positioned for the rest of their journey. It provides not only the full continuum of care, but also a continuum of communication and services as the person's care needs change.

There are two financial components with most CCRCs:

- **The Entrance Fee:** A larger up-front investment much like buying a house. Many people use the equity they have in their home or a portion of it, to fund this Entrance Fee. Like buying a car or a house there is a wide range of prices available. The cost of Entrance Fees can range from $40,000 to over a million dollars! This brings us back to the need to understand how much money your parents have to work with when you start researching. Many communities will offer several ways to make this initial investment. What you'll see most often are:

○ A return offered on the Entrance Fee at the time the resident leaves the community or moves to a higher level of care. It usually ranges anywhere from 50% to 100% of what was originally invested. This is good for people whose financial goal is asset preservation.

○ A lower Entrance Fee that frees up more cash or assets in exchange for a diminishing return on the investment. Usually the return on the Entrance Fee declines at 2% per month over 50 months (just over 4 years) and the resident receives NO return on the Entrance Fee at the time they leave the community. Should the resident leave before the 50-month period, a portion will be returned based on the number months they resided in the community. This is good for people whose financial goal is to minimize the initial investment and free up more money to generate monthly income or support their life style. It is often a preferred choice for people with no children, family or heirs.

• **The Monthly Service Fee:** A Monthly Fee covers all or many of the services and amenities listed in my earlier section on retirement community living. You will find Monthly Fees or Rentals running anywhere from $600 per month for income-qualified retirement communities to over $6,000 per month for large units in upscale retirement communities. Again most retirement communities will include at least the following in that fee or rent:

○ All maintenance to the living unit

○ Utilities (usually excluding phone service)

○ Flexible dining options

○ Housekeeping services

○ Courtesy transportation

○ 24-hour security and emergency response systems

○ Activities that include social, educational, spiritual, cultural and wellness programs

When starting to look at Retirement Communities, especially the CCRC concept, the first thing people want to know is "How much does it cost?" This is not always an easy answer. You will find the cost of the Entrance Fee and Monthly Fee will depend on four things: 1) the size of the unit 2) the amount of long-term care costs that may be wrapped into the contract 3) the financial options offered to pay the Entrance Fee 4) whether there are one or two people residing in the unit.

> The CCRC option is the most complex and confusing to the consumer, yet may offer—for those that can qualify for it on the health and financial parts of the equation—the most comprehensive benefits.

The American Association of Homes and Services for the Aging (AAHSA) is the national organization representing predominantly the not-for-profit sector of the senior housing industry. They have designated three primary types of contracts or Residency Agreement that are the most common in the market place: Type A, Type B, and Type C contracts. However, please note that what I'm giving you here is considered industry "jargon" and if you showed up at a CCRC and asked the marketing person if the community has a Type A or a Type C contract, they might not even know what you are talking about. Again, various programs or contracts are usually called fancy names, like The Traditional, The Platinum Plan, etc., and will vary from community to community.

For simplicity's sake we'll stick with A, B, and C. Starting with an understanding of these contracts will help you more easily understand and process other "hybrids" that you may encounter in your research. The difference between these three types of contracts is this: who pays for a majority of any future long-term care cost? In other words, who is absorbing the financial risk? Is it the resident or the community? Let's review each of the three contracts to more fully understand the concepts.

Type A Contract

Often referred to in the marketplace as "Lifecare", the Type A contract is actually a form of long-term care insurance. This means the community itself functions a little like a long-term care insurance company and absorbs or underwrites a majority of the financial risk for the higher costs of assisted living or skilled nursing care. The bottom line is your parents can get life-long care for about the same cost as the current Monthly Fee of the original independent living unit they invested in. Remember Ethel? If she sold her home and moved into a CCRC under a Type A contract, she would pay an Entrance Fee and then a Monthly Fee. As she aged and her care needs changed, this is what the Type A contract (shaded boxes) would look like compared to the baseline of information we discussed in The Facts of Life section earlier.

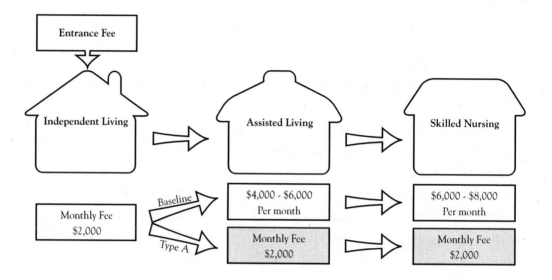

Some communities will also include benevolence or charitable care as part of their contract. This means a person who qualifies financially coming in the door and, through no fault of their own, runs out of money or outlives their assets would not be forced to leave the community. There are financial measures in place for the community to absorb those costs.

The Type A contract provides the maximum risk protection against the high costs of long-term care. Unlike a long-term care policy, there are no elimination periods, maximum time or dollars, etc. Again, it essentially provides unlimited, life-long care at about the same cost as the independent unit that was originally invested in.

What the Type A contract covers:

The cost of a place to live: This is the independent living unit (townhouse, apartment, cottage etc.), assisted living unit (usually a one-bedroom apartment with a small kitchen area) or skilled nursing living unit (usually a bed in a private or semi-private room).

The cost of your meals or a certain meal allowance: Many independent living settings offer a more flexible dining system much like students use in college. Sometimes one meal a day is included in the monthly service fee. Again, there may be variations on this from community to community. In the Assisted Living and Skilled Nursing levels of care, it is usually required by law that three meals a day be served each resident. To cover these extra meals there is sometimes a slight increase in the monthly fee at the time the resident moves to a higher level of care.

24-hour staff support: For the independent setting this usually includes a full staff during business hours, 24-hour security, and a nurse which oversees the wellness and well-being of residents functioning like a geriatric care manager. At the assisted living level of care, a nurse is usually available at least 12 hours a day and there are resident assistants 24 hours a day, so if a resident needs help in the middle of the night, someone is there to assist. The skilled nursing level of care is one notch below a hospital… there are nurses and staff on duty 24/7.

The Type A contract does NOT pay for doctor bills, hospital bills, prescriptions, therapy, bandages, oxygen, and so on. Your parents maintain both their Medicare insurance and their supplemental health insurance policies. Those pay for their health care. The Type A contract helps pay for their long-term care.

The Type B Contract

The Type B contract is sort of a halfway point in sharing financial risk between the A and the C contract. Not all CCRCs will offer this option, but when you encounter it you want to identify it and understand how it positions your parents' risk. Usually the resident receives 60, 90, or 180 days of Assisted Living or Skilled Nursing at little or no additional cost beyond the monthly service fee for your parents' Independent Living unit. Afterward, your parents pay the private pay cost for these higher levels of care, with a 10% discount. Sometimes this plan is referred to as the "60/10 contract option". If Ethel chose a Type B contract it would look like this:

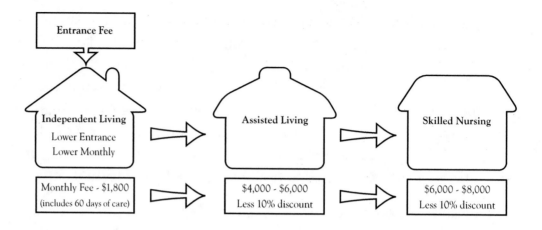

The Type C Contract

In the Type C contract the resident essentially gets the benefits of the CCRC lifestyle without pre-paying for any potential future long-term care costs. This contract is rapidly becoming the most common in the market place. In fact, many new projects are offering only this option.

With the Type C contract your parent(s) have access to the Assisting Living and Skilled Nursing levels of care, they stay on the same campus connected to the community and they only pay the cost of care if and when they need it. This will sometimes be referred as "Fee for Service"… essentially a pay-as-you-go option. It is common for this contract to offer a lower Monthly Fee, as well as higher return on the Entrance Fee. So when Ethel moves on to a higher level of care, the contract she has with Independent Living is completed, and she begins a separate contract for Assisted Living or Skilled Nursing, and pays at the full private pay rate. If Ethel chose a Type C contract it would look like this:

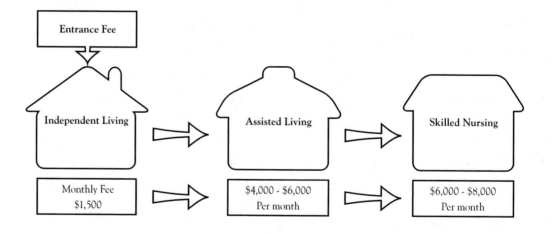

To pay for her higher level of care Ethel would rely on a pool of assets that include:

- The higher return of her Entrance Fee

- Money saved by paying a lower monthly fee during her time in Independent Living

- Her Long Term Care Insurance (if she has it)

- Her remaining assets and income

There are typically three types of people who gravitate to the Type C contract:

- People with long-term care insurance

- People with enough assets who simply wish to "self-insure"

- People who have pre-existing health conditions that fall outside of the underwriting criteria for the Type A contract

Move to a Retirement Community with Limited Services

There are benefits to any retirement community option you explore. Look at all the choices in your parents' geographical area. The community that offers a simpler version of the Rental or Continuing Care Retirement Community providing more limited services may be:

- Move conveniently located closer to family

- Significantly more affordable

- Allow the resident to get more living space for the investment because additional services or "bells and whistles" are not included

- Better meet the overall Risk/Values needs of your parents and family

So there it is. We've just covered the ins-and-outs of the basic options that exist in today's senior housing market. Once you've used the formula to determine the risk/value, health and financial factors affecting you and your parents, you'll likely have focused in on one or two options as an appropriate fit. The next step is starting your research in your targeted geographical area. But first I want to discuss an option that is different than all the above, but can play a significant factor in each of them. We've already touched on it earlier...

Long Term Care Insurance

If you haven't heard of Long Term Care Insurance (LTCI) you should know that it's not Medicare or a supplemental health insurance policy. LTCI helps to pay for the cost of an assisted living community or skilled nursing facility. I mention this option because it is an important tool and growing in popularity and sophistication. However, you should know I am not an expert in long term care insurance. I don't sell insurance or have extensive training in this type of product. What I will do here is cut to the chase and help you grasp a few basics to simplify your research process and how this component may fit into the picture...especially if your parents are considering the benefits of a Type A contract in a Continuing Care Retirement Community. You don't need to be a guru in the field, but you do need to get your head around certain facts to be effective.

When I'm working with people who are looking at my community, one of the first questions I ask is whether Mom or Dad have long term care insurance. If the answer is "yes" or they plan on investing in long term care insurance, then it is important to understand what they're getting for their money. So go find the policy (if they have one) and review it for the following information so you can add this segment to your research.

Elimination period: This is the period of time that they have to be residing in residing in a licensed Assisted Living community or a licensed Skilled Nursing facility before the policy will start to pay out, usually 30, 60, or 90 days. It is common for a policy to have a 90-day elimination period figuring that Medicare and the supplemental health insurance will pay for the first 100 days in a skilled nursing facility. However, remember that Medicare does not pay for assisted living, so the individual has to pay out of pocket for the entire elimination period for assisted living.

Assisted Living and Skilled Nursing: Some older policies only cover a skilled nursing facility and do not cover assisted living. Most new policies will cover both. Look at the policy to be sure you understand exactly what it will cover. If the policy also covers "in home care", that can apply to any independent living setting including an independent living retirement community.

Daily payout: Look at the policy and see where it tells you how much money it will pay out each day. You want to do the simple math to understand how much still has to come out of their pocket even if the policy is paying out. If their long term care insurance pays $80 a day and the cost of skilled nursing is $200 a day...they are still on the hook for $120 a day out of their pocket.

Maximum number of months or dollar amount: Add to the daily payout the length of time it will pay or the total dollar amount it will pay...is it for 2 years, 4 years, unlimited lifetime? This will also figure into both the financial and risk/value equation.

The fine print: Be sure to check for conditions that the policy will NOT cover.

Monthly or annual premiums: What does the policy cost?

Inflation clause: Does the policy have an inflation clause that automatically increases the amount of the daily payout over the years? Assisted living and skilled nursing care costs usually increase 4 to 6% or more on an annual basis. If the policy does not have the inflation clause, the amount it pays out will have diminishing impact and increase the financial risk.

Weigh cost/benefits to Type A CCRC contract: If they are thinking about purchasing long term care insurance or considering making a move to a retirement community, you want to include the financial comparison of the Type A contract which I discussed earlier.

Work with a specialist: If your parents are starting to look at long term care insurance as a way to position their risk for the future assisted living or skilled nursing costs, be sure to consult with a professional who specializes in this area of insurance. It is also wise to evaluate more than one company's products. My husband and I opted to work with a broker who showed us five or six different companies before we whittled it down between three and then made our final decision. If they already have insurance, contact the company and confirm the details of their policy BEFORE they start researching retirement community options. It will save lots of time!

Notes:

Key Points to Remember…

- Those who choose to stay in their own home need to have a support system in place should their independence decline.

- If you're considering downsizing within traditional Real Estate, be sure to consider if another move is a possibility in a few years.

- If you have the right family dynamics, moving in with family can be a very rewarding experience.

- Remember that the typical Active Adult Community is aimed at the 55 to 60 year old crowd.

- Rental Retirement Communities and Retirement Communities with limited services can be much more cost-effective than Continuing Care Retirement Communities, but with fewer benefits.

- Be sure to understand the Type A, B, and C contracts of a CCRC. You will see them under many other names.

- Long Term Care Insurance can pay for the costs of Assisted Living or Skilled Nursing. Be sure you understand the policy.

Research Notes

The following steps can be taken in nearly any order. When put to use, they will help you sort the wheat from the chaff and key into the information that matters most when making an important decision like this. Be sure to start early because it will only make things easier.

1. Research the financial strength and stability of the parent corporation
Just as you would do before making any major investment, be sure to research the financial aspects of the organization. It is entirely appropriate to ask for a financial report about the parent corporation of a community you're researching. Some communities are religiously affiliated, others are hospital affiliated, and some are a community partnership project or a publicly traded for-profit corporation. However the organization is structured, your parents must feel comfortable and confident with the fiscal integrity of the community and the organization that stands behind it.

2. Look at the ratios
If your research will include looking at a Continuing Care Retirement Community (CCRC) or any retirement community that offers higher levels of care beyond independent living, always ask about the ratios…that is, how many independent units do they have compared to the number of assisted living units and skilled nursing beds? The industry standard is typically about 1:5. So if a community boasts 500 apartment homes and only has 25 assisted living units and 30 beds in their skilled nursing center, you want to know what would happen if your parents

had a need and all those units/beds were occupied. This is something that many people overlook up front, and only when they have a need that cannot be met do they begin to understand how critical this can be. At the very least, if a potential problem exists, you simply want to be aware of it up front and be comfortable with the alternative way of meeting their needs that the community would provide.

3. Historical patterns for fee increases

Regardless of where your parents go or what community they choose (even if they stay at home) you can expect the monthly fee or rent will increase each year. That's just the way it is. What the savvy consumer needs to ask is, "What is the historical pattern of your monthly fee/rent increases?" The answer will not only tell you what to expect in the future if your parents lived in that community, but will also provide insight into the financial stability of the organization.

Standard annual increases in the independent living industry are 3 to 6%. If a community had a 10% increase one year, or maybe issued two increases within one calendar year, it may indicate financial instability. Don't be fooled by a community that claims they will never increase their fees. A promise like that may sound good to the consumer, but the reality is a retirement community is a business like any other, and it can't stay in business by absorbing all the cost increases to deliver their products and services. A community that does this will eventually run into financial problems that could be far worse for the residents than if they had paid a small increase in fees each year. So go into your research accepting the fee increases as the nature of the beast; just inquire into the historical pattern looking for consistency over the years.

4. The people and the culture

After you get past what I call the "bricks and mortar" part of the search—the geographic location, the costs, the appearance, timing the move, and so on—your parents must focus on the people and the culture of the community. Every community will have wonderful people and a unique culture, and your parents must find the best fit for themselves. All the concerns they may have about costs, programs, activities, dining, and where to put their loveseat or favorite chair…those things will pass. And when they do, it is the people of the community that will determine how happy your parents will be with their new lifestyle.

As part of your research, be sure to include your parents having lunch or dinner in the dining room and interacting with people who live in the community. Take advantage of social events where they can meet and visit with residents. Some communities also offer an opportunity to stay in their guest suite for a few nights, participating in the life of the community to get a sense of the people and culture. If you or your parents know someone already living in the community, talk to them! However, be sure to focus on this level of research AFTER you have obtained the financial details, taken a tour, and know the community is of strong interest to your parents.

5. Tour the continuum of care

If your parents are evaluating a community that offers other levels of care, such as assisted living, memory loss, or skilled nursing care, be sure to take a tour of these higher levels of care. Put a visual to it. See what the Assisted Living area looks like. What is their sense of things when they walk through the Skilled Nursing area? I've had clients that refuse to look at these levels of care because it is a way of denying anything could ever happen to them. I always encourage families to take this step so everyone is comfortable with the entire picture up front.

If your parents are looking at an independent living retirement community with no higher levels of care, an Active Adult Community, a move to traditional real estate, or deciding to stay in their home, then do the research into assisted living and skilled care that may exist in the area. It's good to have an idea of where they would want to live if there was a crisis. As uncomfortable as it can be, when an elderly parent chooses some options it is a great gift to the family members that will have to help them though any potential crisis, especially if those family members live outside the area and don't know what is near by.

6. Compare apples to apples

This is a very common challenge for people just starting their research (though hopefully easier for you after reading this book!). Be sure you are zeroed in on the correct level of care. Take a close look at the health part of the formula and if you feel it could be borderline between independent living and assisted living, start by exploring one of each and asking guidance from their staff clinician, if available.

The biggest challenge is comparing CCRC communities, understanding their various contracts, and comparing each one's return on investment. You must consider services, future care, financial terms, the product, and the people. It's more than just shopping for a pair of black shoes!

Most times a community will market their programs with a different name for the various programs or contract types…the Classic Plan, the Gold Level, the Traditional Program. When you read a bit further you'll find they usually translate into a Type A, B, or C contract. Be sure to review the previous sections on contract types as you sift through a community's jargon so you clearly understand what the community is offering. In different parts of the country you may run into some variations, but understanding the basics we've covered will help you discern any differences.

7. Put your thoughts and feelings on paper
I know this sounds so logical and simple…and it is! It's also incredibly useful. Yet people still resist doing this. When you next go out to visit a community, try this exercise.

Take a piece of paper and put the name of the community on the top. Draw a line down the middle and put a plus sign on one side, and a minus sign on the other. As soon as you and your parents finish the visit and get into the car to leave, start a "brain dump" of everything you heard and saw…right there in the parking lot. Just get it on paper! If there's anything you're not sure about, put a question mark next to it and figure out which column it should go in later. Now, visit five communities, and do this exercise for each one. Then line up the papers on the dining room table and look at the + signs and – signs. I guarantee you'll see patterns.

This has a couple of excellent benefits. For starters, it brings some logic into a very emotionally charged process. And if you spread your research out over time, it helps you remember which community had the washer and dryer in the apartments, which one had the eat-in kitchen or the opera lecture group that sounded so exciting. Capture as much as you can on paper for further reflection in your mind. To get you started I've included some helpful worksheets in the back. If you are a computer whiz, put it on a spreadsheet!

8. Support from family, friends, legal or financial counsel
Gathering and processing this information can be exhausting and

sometimes overwhelming. It helps to have at least one other person to share in the research. I find families often have someone that's the left-brained, analytical "numbers" person, and someone else who is in tune with the "softer side"…the emotions, desires, preferences, and so on. Having this kind of a small and balanced team comes in handy.

The flip side of the coin is having five siblings and their spouses all show up with mom to look at a community…everyone has different opinions, different tastes, and a different vision of what mom wants or needs. I remember working with Marian, who came for a second visit to choose an apartment with all her children and their spouses. Poor Marian couldn't get a word in edgewise and the children each wanted her to have the largest apartment. Later she turned to me and quietly said, "I don't want that much space, I really prefer the smaller one."

Some families will need "role reversal". I've worked with adult children who will insist every decision be made by the parent and will not offer their opinions. It's common for the aging parent to become a little bit like the child, actually wanting and needing direction from their adult children…hoping they will tell them (gently and firmly) what is best for them and what the family wants them to do. I've also worked with aging parents that manage the entire process on their own, and only when it's a done deal do they tell their children or family.

In addition to family, many people feel more comfortable having their attorney review contracts for them, or consult with their financial planner when evaluating the various financial options. Do whatever feels the most comfortable. Get all the paperwork in advance and have someone you trust review it with you and get all your questions answered.

9. Make sure you understand details

Let's face it, contractual details can be boring. Like buying a new house, most people are usually more concerned with what color to paint the bedroom, what furniture to bring, making new friends or weeding out years of "stuff" than they are with the details of the papers at closing. Nonetheless, make sure both you and your parents understand the contractual details and make notes for future reference. Any area concerning the life of the community that are important to them—pets, the woodshop, the greenhouse, religious services, dress codes, policies on serving alcohol, use of common spaces—be sure to get the information and details up front. As tedious as it can be sometimes, be organized with the paperwork, because you or your parents will end up needing to refer back to it years from the time they move into a community.

10. Explore! Experience! Enjoy!

Have fun with the research process. Some people spend years slowly gathering information, meeting with people, looking at options, attending events at different communities while the answers gradually reveal themselves. When a person tells me "I just don't know what I'm going to do!" I tell them, "Of course you don't...how can you? You must go out there and learn, expose yourself to the options, talk to people, experience various communities and lifestyles."

Be honest with yourself and others. If a community is way out of reach financially, or not a geographical possibility, cross it off the list and focus on options that are possible. Even if your parents are not ready to make a decision or a move now, it is still appropriate and expected by communities that you'll visit, learn and enjoy the hospitality they may offer. I encourage you and your parents to explore, experience and enjoy the research journey!

You Made It!

Congratulations… you're now a savvy consumer of senior housing. Before you read this book you may have been thinking, "Where do I start? What's out there? How will I find the time?" Hopefully those questions have been answered to some degree. Consider for a moment what you've learned:

- You know the signs to look for that indicate it's time for your parents to make a change
- You know the three big questions they tend to ask themselves
- You understand the progression of elder care from Independent Living to Assisted Living to Skilled Nursing Care
- You know the typical costs associated with those levels of care, and the role of Medicare and Medicaid
- You understand how our paradigms and perceptions can influence our judgment, and how to keep an open mind
- You know the formula for success: Risks and Values + Health + Finances = Your Best Option and how the three factors play into your research and focus your options
- You have an arsenal of questions and "conversation starters" to help get your parents talking about their next steps
- You understand the basic senior housing options and the pros and cons of each
- You have several specific actions you can take to jumpstart your research

All in all, you've come a long way since opening this book. I once read that "The art of living lies in a fine mingling of letting go and holding on". As you launch into your research, you'll find this is especially true in transitioning to a senior housing lifestyle. Best of luck and enjoy your journey!

Glossary

Assisted Living: A special retirement community designed for older adults who need assistance with one or more Activities of Daily Living (ADLs) i.e. getting dressed, bathing, remembering to take medications, etc. This lifestyle is often referred to as "independent living with assistive services". It meets the needs of people who do not need 24-hour nursing care, yet cannot successfully live in an independent setting.

Continuing Care Retirement Community (CCRC): This refers to a retirement community that provides independent living, assisted living, and skilled nursing services all on one campus or in one building.

Continuum of Care: Another term used when referring to the three lifestyles in a continuing care retirement community. i.e. "We have access to the full continuum of care."

Entrance Fee: This term is sometimes referred to as the "buy-in" or the "endowment". The Entrance Fee most often applies to the CCRC type of community and equates to buying a house. There are usually different options available for the return of the Entrance Fee or a portion of it, depending on which financial option the consumer chooses. These may be different in every community. It is important to understand your options and what you get for the money you invest.

Lifecare: A term used when referring to a Continuing Care Retirement Community that financially underwrites a portion of the cost of a person's long term care needs.

Long Term Care Insurance: This is an insurance policy designed to help offset the costs for Assisted Living and/or Skilled Nursing Care. It is NOT health insurance.

Monthly Service Fee: This term equates to what it costs to live in your home. It will bundle together a wide variety of services, which may differ slightly in each community, but usually include property taxes, maintenance, utilities, dining services, housekeeping, security, activities, transportation etc. The monthly services will be very similar in the Rental Community and CCRC, except Long Term Care services will be included in this Monthly Fee for the type A and B contracts used in a CCRC.

Ratios: This refers to the number of units for independent living within a CCRC and how that number compares to the total number of units in the continuum of care. Example: 500 apartments for independent living, 25 units for assisted living, 50 units for skilled nursing care (500 /75) would NOT be favorable ratios. Your concern as a consumer is that a CCRC has sufficient space available to handle the aging-in-place process with enough available units in the continuum of care.

Residency Agreement: The primary legal document signed by the resident(s) when moving into a Continuing Care Retirement Community. There are three types of contracts most frequently used in a CCRC.

Type A Contract: Often referred to as a "full lifecare" contract, this type of contract provides maximum risk protection. It is a form of Long Term Care Insurance where the resident receives life-long care for about the same cost as the current Monthly Service Fee in their independent unit throughout the entire continuum of care. In some CCRC communities, this type of contract may also include a charitable care clause. A medical approval is required. Much like an insurance company, the CCRC is assessing a risk (the applicant's health and financial resources) and determining if they will underwrite the cost of their long-term care for the rest of their lives.

Type B Contract: Often referred to as a "modified lifecare" contract, this type of contract provides the resident with a certain number of days of care throughout the continuum of care…usually 30, 60, 90 or 180 days. After the specified number of days has been utilized, the resident pays the private pay rates for assisted living and skilled nursing care usually receiving a 10% discount. Because the CCRC is not absorbing as much financial risk to pay for long term care costs, the consumer will usually see lower Entrance Fees and lower Monthly Fees for the B contract as compared to the A contract.

Type C Contract: Often referred to as a "fee for service" contract, this type of contract provides the resident with all the advantages of the CCRC lifestyle, but does not include any financial underwriting when people access the continuum of care. It is essentially a "pay as you go…if and when you need the higher levels of care". Usually this type of contract will provide lower Monthly Fees and a higher return on the Entrance Fee because there is no financial risk on the part of the community.

Skilled Nursing Facility: Often referred to as a nursing home, this type of community is designed to provide the highest level of care for individuals requiring a registered nurse and care 24 hours a day. Some, but not all, skilled nursing facilities are certified for Medicare and Medicaid.

Worksheets

After gathering all this information you'll have a good idea of what it is costing your parents to maintain their current lifestyle. This understanding will also play into your Risk & Values conversations.

Current Lifestyle Costs

Home Maintenance

    House Cleaning $ _____

    Lawn Care $ _____

    Tree and Shrub Care $ _____

    Gutter Cleaning $ _____

    Snow Removal $ _____

    Painting and Repairs (interior and exterior) $ _____

    Roof, Windows, Siding, Sump Pump, etc. $ _____

    Trash and Garbage Removal $ _____

    Major Appliances Maintain/Replace

        Furnace $ _____

        Air Conditioning $ _____

        Water Heater $ _____

        Other $ _____

Property Tax $ _____

Homeowner's Insurance $ _____

Food $ _____

Security Systems $ _____

Cable or Satellite TV Service $ _____

Long Term Care Insurance $ _____

Health Insurance $ _____

Other $ _____

Total Cost to Maintain Current Lifestyle $ _____

Income and Asset Calculator

Monthly Income	1st Person	2nd Person
Social Security	$ _____	$ _____
Pension *(Sole Survivor _____ %)*	$ _____	$ _____
Dividends	$ _____	$ _____
Interest	$ _____	$ _____
Mortgage / Rental Income	$ _____	$ _____
IRA Income	$ _____	$ _____
Trust Income	$ _____	$ _____
Other Income	$ _____	$ _____
Total Monthly Income	$ _____	$ _____

Capital Assets

Capital Assets		Liabilities	
Cash *(Savings & Checking)*	$ _____	Real Estate	$ _____
Stocks and Bonds	$ _____	Auto	$ _____
CDs	$ _____	Loan Guarantees	$ _____
IRAs	$ _____	Credit Cards	$ _____
Annuities	$ _____	Other	$ _____
Money Markets	$ _____	**Total Liabilities**	$ _____
Real Estate	$ _____		
Trust Fund	$ _____		
Investment Life Insurance	$ _____		
Other	$ _____		
Total Combined Assets	$ _____		

Net Assets (Assets – Liabilities) $ _____

Quick Summary & Financial Reference for Researching

Total Assets $ _____

Total "Available" Monthly Income $ _____

Name of Community/Option

+   **−**

Name of Community/Option

+

−

Name of Community/Option

+

−

Name of Community/Option

+   **−**

Name of Community/Option

+

−

Name of Community/Option

+

−

Additional Resources

www.AAHSA.org

The American Association for Homes and Services for the Aging

www.ALFA.org

Assisted Living Federation of America

www.AlternativesForSeniors.com

A semi-annual senior housing directory listing retirement communities, assisted living and skilled nursing facilities

www.APlaceForMom.com

A free referral service helping families find nursing homes, assisted living, Alzheimer's care, retirement communities, and home care

www.ASilverConnection.com

A free senior housing referral service for independent, CCRC, assisted living, memory care, skilled nursing, or in-home care

www.ElderIndustry.com

The website for the Joy Loverde's book, The Complete Eldercare Planner, a comprehensive, all-in-one resource on eldercare

www.NewLifestyles.com

A comprehensive on-line, nationwide housing directory and research tool

www.Paxem.com

Senior relocation experts that assist with downsizing, organizing, de-cluttering, preparing a home for sale, packing, managing the move, and setting up the new home

www.SeniorDirectory.com

The website for a senior directory called Senior Resource Guide providing resources for senior housing, home health, professional, health and other senior services

www.SeniorResourceGuide.com

SeniorsResourceGuide.com is the website of the Senior Blue Book. Both groups work together to bring valuable information and resources to seniors and adult children

www.SeniorHousingNet.com

An on-line resource for finding senior housing and care

www.SeniorOutlook.com

An after 55 housing and resource guide

www.SeniorSites.com

A comprehensive web source of non-profit housing and services for seniors

Acknowledgments

To my husband Fritz and son Gabe,
thank you for your love, encouragement, partnership,
support, and steadfast belief in our project.

To my mother, Mary Schultz and mother-in-law, Hilda Gloege,
thank you for graciously sharing your stories so that others may learn.

To Joe Benson and Phyllis Thornton,
thank you for being a friend over the years, for your mentorship,
guidance, and coaching as I continue to learn.

Mission Statement

Empowering individuals with knowledge, insight and resources to
successfully navigate lifestyle and aging transitions.

About Randalynn Kaye

As the director of marketing for a highly-regarded senior living community in suburban Chicago, Randalynn Kaye has worked with and counseled hundreds of people searching various senior lifestyle options. She is actively involved with the American Association of Homes and Services for the Aging (AAHSA) and Life Services Network (LSN), as well as the Assisted Living Federation of America (ALFA). A sought-after speaker, Kaye is regularly interviewed for her expertise on issues facing today's seniors and their families. She has been featured as a senior specialist in major media including *USA Weekend, Christian Science Monitor, Chicago Tribune*, and Superstation WGN, to name a few.

Kaye is also the adult child of aging parents. In 2005, she helped her husband's parents through tough family conversations, research, the decision-making process and eventual move from their home of 50 years. And in 2006, when a severe stroke left her own father needing serious care, she managed his transition, eventually moving her parents into her own house, as they prepared to move to a retirement community nearby. With the help of her family, she then handled the continued decline of her father's health, hospice, his death and ultimately, helping her mother move on with life—learning lessons no one truly understands until they've experienced the process first-hand.

An author, speaker, and consultant, Randalynn lives with her husband in St. Charles, Illinois. *Senior Housing 101* is also available as an e-Book at www.Elder-Transitions.com. Randalynn welcomes your comments and messages at RK@Elder-Transitions.com.